I0003654

AWS DeepLens Developer Guide

A catalogue record for this book is available from the Hong Kong Public Libraries.

Published in Hong Kong by Samurai Media Limited.

Email: info@samuraimedia.org

ISBN 9789888408429

Contents

What Is AWS DeepLens?

Welcome to the *AWS DeepLens Developer Guide*. AWS DeepLens is a wireless video camera and API. It shows you how to use the latest Artificial Intelligence (AI) tools and technology to develop computer vision applications. Through examples and tutorials, AWS DeepLens gives you hands-on experience using a physical camera to run real-time computer vision models.

The AWS DeepLens camera, or device, uses deep convolutional neural networks (CNNs) to analyze visual imagery. You use the device as a development environment to build computer vision applications.

AWS DeepLens works with the following AWS services:

- Amazon SageMaker, for model training and validation

- AWS Lambda, for running inference against CNN models

- AWS Greengrass, for deploying updates and functions to your device

Get started with AWS DeepLens by using any of the pretrained models that come with your device. As you become proficient, you can develop, train, and deploy your own models.

- AWS DeepLens Hardware
- Supported Frameworks
- How AWS DeepLens Works
- Are You an AWS DeepLens First-time User?
- More Info

AWS DeepLens Hardware

The AWS DeepLens camera includes the following:

- A 4-megapixel camera with MJPEG (Motion JPEG)

- 8 GB of on-board memory

- 16 GB of storage capacity

- A 32-GB SD (Secure Digital) card

- WiFi support for both 2.4 GHz and 5 GHz standard dual-band networking

- A micro HDMI display port

- Audio out and USB ports

The AWS DeepLens camera is powered by an Intel® Atomprocessor, which can process 100 billion floating-point operations per second (GFLOPS). This gives you all of the compute power that you need to perform inference on your device. The micro HDMI display port, audio out, and USB ports allow you to attach peripherals, so you can get creative with your computer vision applications.

You can use AWS DeepLens as soon as you register it. Begin by deploying a sample project, and use it as an example for developing your own computer vision applications.

Supported Frameworks

Currently, AWS DeepLens supports only the Apache MXNet framework and Gluon models. For more information, see Machine Learning Frameworks Supported by AWS DeepLens.

How AWS DeepLens Works

The following diagram illustrates how AWS DeepLens works.

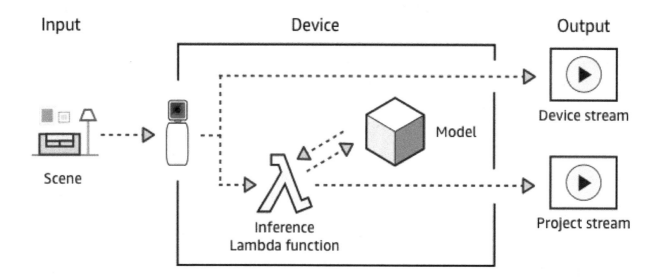

1. When turned on, the AWS DeepLens captures a video stream.

2. Your AWS DeepLens produces two output streams:

   - **Device stream**—The video stream passed through without processing

   - **Project stream**—The results of the model's processing video frames

     1. The Inference Lambda function receives unprocessed video frames.

     2. The Inference Lambda function passes the unprocessed frames to the project's deep learning model, where they are processed.

     3. The Inference Lambda function receives the processed frames from the model and passes the processed frames on in the project stream.

        ```
        Infinite inference is running. Sample result of the last frame is
        label     prob
        794    0.681035220623
        669    0.0477042198181
        905    0.0444286055863
        564    0.0426452308893
        706    0.0312749966979
        ```

For more information, see Viewing AWS DeepLens Project Output.

Are You an AWS DeepLens First-time User?

If you are a first-time AWS DeepLens user, we recommend that you do the following in order:

1. **Read How AWS DeepLens Works**—Explains AWS DeepLens and how to use it to develop computer vision applications.

2. **Explore Amazon SageMaker**—Explains some of the basic functionality of Amazon SageMaker. AWS DeepLens uses Amazon SageMaker to build and train CNN models. You use Amazon SageMaker to create your own AWS DeepLens models and projects.

3. **Learn about the AWS DeepLens Device Library**—The device library describes the classes and methods that you can use in your Lambda functions.

4. **Perform the tasks in Getting Started with AWS DeepLens**—Set up your AWS account, create the AWS Identity and Access Management (IAM) permissions and roles that you need to run AWS DeepLens, and register and set up your AWS DeepLens device.

   After you've set up your AWS DeepLens environment and device, begin using it by trying these exercises:

   1. **Creating and Deploying an AWS DeepLens Sample Project**—Walks you through creating sample AWS DeepLens project, which is included with your device.

   2. **Editing an Existing Model with Amazon SageMaker**—Walks you through creating and training a model using Amazon SageMaker.

   3. **Extending any Project's Functionality**—Walks you through taking output from your AWS DeepLens and using it to trigger an action.

More Info

- AWS DeepLens Forum

Getting Started with AWS DeepLens

Before using AWS DeepLens, register your device, connect it, set it up, and verify that it's connected. The following graphic shows where you perform each step.

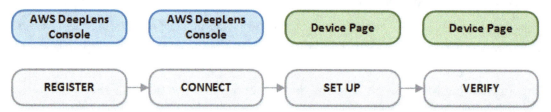

- Prerequisites
- Register Your AWS DeepLens Device
- Connect AWS DeepLens to the Network
- Set Up Your AWS DeepLens Device
- Verify That Your AWS DeepLens Is Connected

Prerequisites

Before you can begin using AWS DeepLens, you need an AWS account and an IAM user.

Create an AWS Account

To use AWS services, you need an AWS account. If you don't have one, create one now.

The AWS account is free. You pay only for the AWS services that you use.

To create an AWS account

1. Go to https://portal.aws.amazon.com.

2. Choose **Create a Free Account**.

3. Follow the instructions on the page.

   Part of the sign-up process involves receiving a phone call and entering a PIN using the phone keypad.

Create an IAM User

You use the AWS Identity and Access Management (IAM) user to specify to whom the IAM policies and roles apply.

Important
Record your **Access Key** and **Secret Key**. You need them to make calls with the AWS CLI.

To create an IAM user

1. Sign in to the AWS Management Console and open the IAM console at https://console.aws.amazon.com/iam/.

2. In the navigation pane, choose **Users**, then choose **Add user**.

3. For **Access type**, choose both **Programmatic Access** and **AWS Management Console Access**.

4. For **Console password**, choose **Autogenerated password** or **Custom password**. If you choose **Custom password**, type a password.

5. Choose whether to require the user to reset the password at the next sign-in, then choose **Next: Permissions**.

6. For **Set permissions for** , choose **Attach existing policies directly**, **AdministrativeAccess**, and **Next: Review**.

7. Review the settings. To return to the previous page to make changes, choose **Previous**. To create the user, choose **Create user**.

Now that you have an AWS account and IAM user, continue to Register Your AWS DeepLens Device.

Register Your AWS DeepLens Device

Use your computer's browser to register your device and download a certificate.

Before you continue, complete the Prerequisites.

To register AWS DeepLens

1. Sign in to the AWS Management Console and open the AWS DeepLens console at https://console.aws. amazon.com/deeplens/home?region=us-east-1#firstrun.

2. Choose **Register device**.

3. For **Device name**, type a name for your AWS DeepLens, then choose **Next**.

   Use only alphanumeric characters and dashes (-).

4. If this is your first time registering an AWS DeepLens device, create the following AWS Identity and Access Management (IAM) roles. They give AWS DeepLens the permissions it needs to perform tasks on your behalf.

   If you have already created these roles, skip to step 5.

   1. **IAM role for AWS DeepLens**

      From the list, choose **AWSDeepLensServiceRole**. If **AWSDeepLensServiceRole** isn't listed, choose **Create role in IAM** and follow these steps in the IAM console.

      1. Accept the **DeepLens** service and **DeepLens** use case by choosing **Next: Permissions**.

      2. Accept the **AWSDeepLensServiceRolePolicy** policy by choosing **Next: Review**.

      3. Accept the role name **AWSDeepLensServiceRole** and the provided description by choosing **Create role**. Do not change the role name.

      4. Close the IAM window.

   2. **IAM role for AWS Greengrass service**

      From the list, choose **AWSDeepLensGreengrassRole**. If **AWSDeepLensGreengrassRole** isn't listed, choose **Create role in IAM** and follow these steps in the IAM console.

      1. Accept the **Greengrass** service and **Greengrass** use case by choosing **Next: Permissions**.

      2. Accept the **AWSGreengrassResourceAccessRolePolicy** policy by choosing **Next: Review**.

      3. Accept the role name **AWSDeepLensGreengrassRole** and the provided description by choosing **Create role**. Do not change the role name.

      4. Close the IAM window.

   3. **IAM role for AWS Greengrass device groups**.

      From the list, choose **AWSDeepLensGreengrassGroupRole**. If **AWSDeepLensGreengrass-GroupRole** isn't listed, choose **Create role in IAM** and follow these steps in the IAM console.

      1. Accept the **DeepLens** service and the **DeepLens - Greengrass Lambda** use case by choosing **Next: Permissions**.

      2. Accept the **AWSDeepLensLambdaFunctionAccessPolicy** policy by choosing **Next: Review**.

      3. Accept the role name **AWSDeepLensGreengrassGroupRole** and the provided description by choose **Create role**. Do not change the role name.

      4. Close the IAM window.

4. **IAM role for Amazon SageMaker**

   From the list, choose **AWSDeepLensSagemakerRole**. If **AWSDeepLensSagemakerRole** isn't listed, choose **Create role in IAM** and follow these steps in the IAM console.

   1. Accept the **SageMaker** service and the **SageMaker - Execution** use case by choosing **Next: Permissions**.

   2. Accept the **AmazonSageMakerFullAccess** policy by choosing **Next: Review**.

   3. Accept the role name **AWSDeepLensSageMakerRole** and the provided description by choosing **Create role**. Do not change the role name.

   4. Close the IAM window.

5. **IAM role for AWS Lambda**

   From the list, choose **AWSDeepLensLambdaRole**. If **AWSDeepLensLambdaRole** isn't listed, choose **Create role in IAM** and follow these steps i the IAM console.

   1. Accept the **Lambda** service and the **Lambda** use case by choosing **Next: Permissions**.

   2. Accept the **AWSLambdaFullAccess** policy by choosing **Next: Review**.

   3. Accept the role name **AWSDeepLensLambdaRole** and the provided description by choosing **Create role**. Do not change the role name.

   4. Close the IAM window.

5. In AWS DeepLens, on the **Set permissions** page, choose **Refresh IAM roles**, then do the following:

   - For **IAM role for AWS DeepLens**, choose **AWSDeepLensServiceRole**.

   - For **IAM role for AWS Greengrass service**, choose **AWSDeepLensGreengrassRole**.

   - For **IAM role for AWS Greengrass device groups**, choose **AWSDeepLensGreegrassGroup-Role**.

   - For **IAM role for Amazon SageMaker**, choose **AWSDeepLensSagemakerRole**.

   - For **IAM role for AWS Lambda**, choose **AWSDeepLensLambdaRole**. **Important** Attach the roles exactly as described. Otherwise, you might have trouble deploying models to AWS DeepLens. If any of the lists do not have the specified role, find that role in step 4, follow the directions to create the role, choose **Refresh IAM roles**, and return to where you were in step 5.

6. Choose **Next**.

7. On the **Download certificate** page, choose **Download certificate**, then choose **Save File**. Note where you save the certificate file because you need it later.

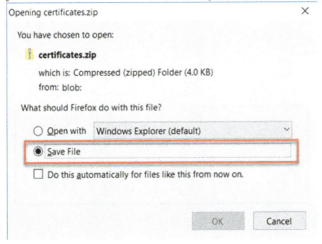

11

After the certificate has been downloaded, choose **Register. Important**
The certificate is a .zip file. You attach it to AWS DeepLens in .zip format, so don't unzip it.
Certificates aren't reusable. You need to generate a new certificate every time you register your device.

Connect AWS DeepLens to the Network

Before you can use AWS DeepLens, you have to connect it to the network.

To connect to your AWS DeepLens

1. Start your AWS DeepLens device by plugging the power cord into an outlet and the other end into the back of your device. Turn on the AWS DeepLens by pressing the On/Off button on the front of the device.

2. On your computer, choose the SSID for your AWS DeepLens from the list of available networks. The SSID and password are on the bottom of your device.

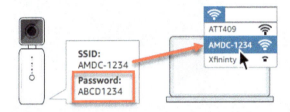

   When prompted, type the AWS DeepLens password.

Set Up Your AWS DeepLens Device

Use your computer to set up your AWS DeepLens device.

To set up your device

1. In a browser, open a new tab and navigate to http://192.168.0.1.

2. On the **Device** page:

    1. Connect to the network.

       Choose your local network, type the password, then choose **Next**. If you are using Ethernet to connect to AWS DeepLens, choose the Ethernet option.

    2. Upload the certificate.

       Locate and choose the certificate that you downloaded from the AWS DeepLens console, then choose **Upload certificate**.

       The certificate is saved as a .zip file in your `Downloads` directory. Don't unzip the file. You attach the certificate as a .zip file.

    3. Configure device access.

        1. **Create a password for the device**—You need this password to access and update your AWS DeepLens.

        2. SSH server—We recommend disabling SSH. SSH allows you to log in without using the AWS DeepLens console.

        3. **Automatic updates**—We recommend enabling this option. Enabling automatic updates keeps your device's software up-to-date.

    4. Review the settings and finish setting up the device.

       To modify settings, choose **Edit** for the setting that you want to change.

       Choose **Finish**.

Verify That Your AWS DeepLens Is Connected

After you set up your device, your computer automatically connects to the internet. This can take a few seconds. When your device is connected, you see the following message:

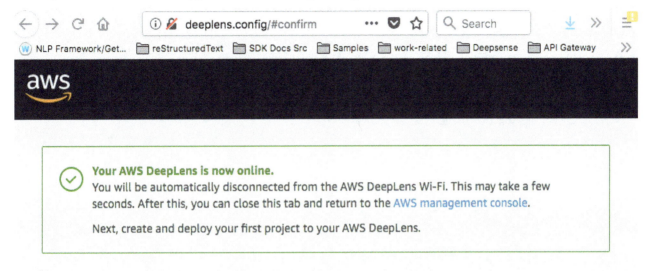

After the connection is established, you can return to the AWS DeepLens console. You are now ready to deploy an AWS DeepLens project. For more information, see Creating and Deploying an AWS DeepLens Sample Project.

If you fail to establish a connection, return to Connect AWS DeepLens to the Network and repeat the steps for setting up your device and connecting it to the network.

Working with AWS DeepLens Projects

When your AWS DeepLens device is registered and connected, you can begin using it. To use your device for deep learning, you create a project and deploy it to your AWS DeepLens device. An AWS DeepLens *project* is made up of deep learning models and associated AWS Lambda functions.

AWS DeepLens comes with several sample projects that you can deploy and use right out of the box.

- Machine Learning Frameworks Supported by AWS DeepLens
- Deploying an AWS DeepLens Project
- Viewing AWS DeepLens Project Output
- Working with AWS DeepLens Sample Projects
- Working with AWS DeepLens Custom Projects

Machine Learning Frameworks Supported by AWS DeepLens

Currently, AWS DeepLens supports only models created with the Apache MXNet framework.

- Apache MXNet Models
- Gluon Models

Apache MXNet Models

AWS DeepLens supports the following MXNet layers.

Supported MXNet Layers
Activation
BatchNorm
Concat
_contrib_MultiBoxDetection
_contrib_MultiBoxPrior
Convolution
Deconvolution
elemwise_add
Flatten
FullyConnected
InputLayer
L2Norm
LRN (Local Response Normalization)
Pooling
Reshape
ScaleShift
SoftmaxActivation
SoftmaxOutput
transpose
UpSampling
_mul
_Plus

For more information about MXNet, see Apache MXNet.

Gluon Models

Gluon is an API within MXNet that you use to access MXNet models.

Example
The following example shows how to export your Squeezenet version 1 model using the Gluon API. The output is a symbol and params file with 'squeezenet' as the filename prefix.

```
1 import mxnet as mx
2 from mxnet.gluon.model_zoo import vision
3 squeezenet = vision.squeezenet_v1(pretrained=True, ctx=mx.cpu())
4
5 # to export you need to hybridize your gluon model
6 squeezenet.hybridize()
7
```

```
8  # 'squeezenets input pattern is images 224x224, so prep a fake image
9  fake_image = mx.nd.random.uniform(shape=(1,3,224,224), ctx=mx.cpu())
10
11 # run the model once
12 result = squeezenet(fake_image)
13
14 # now you can export it; you can use a path if desired 'models/'squeezenet
15 squeezenet.export'(squeezenet')
```

The following table lists the AWS DeepLens supported models from the Gluon model zoo.

Supported Gluon Models	Model	Description
AlexNet	Image classification model trained on the ImageNet dataset from ONNX	
MobileNet	Image classification model trained in TensorFlow using RMSprop	
ResNet	Image classification model trained on the ImageNet dataset from MXNet	
SqueezeNet	Image classification model trained on the ImageNet dataset from ONNX	
VGG	Image classification model trained on ImageNet dataset imported from MXNet or ONNX	

* Currently, AWS DeepLens doesn't support the Gluon DenseNet or Inception models.

For a complete list of models and more information, see the following:

- Gluon
- Gluon Model Zoo

Deploying an AWS DeepLens Project

In this walkthrough, you deploy the Object Detection project. The Object Detection project analyzes images within a video stream on your AWS DeepLens device to identify objects. It can recognize as many as 20 types of objects. The steps to deploying any AWS DeepLens project are the same as we use here to deploy the Object Detection project.

Your web browser is the interface between you and your AWS DeepLens device. You perform all of the following activities on your browser after logging on to AWS:

1. On the **Projects** screen, choose the radio button to the left of your project name, then choose **Deploy to device**.

2. On the **Target device** screen, from the list of AWS DeepLens devices, choose the radio button to the left of the device that you want to deploy this project to. An AWS DeepLens device can have only one project deployed to it at a time.

3. Choose **Review**.

   If a project is already deployed to the device, you will see an error message that deploying this project will overwrite the project that is already running on the device. Choose **Continue project**.

   This will take you to the **Review and deploy** screen.

4. On the **Review and deploy** screen, review your project and choose either **Previous** to go back and make changes, or **Deploy** to deploy the project. **Important**
   Deploying a project incurs costs for the AWS services that are used to run the project.

For instructions on viewing your project's output, see Viewing AWS DeepLens Project Output.

Viewing AWS DeepLens Project Output

AWS DeepLens produces two output streams: the device stream and a project stream. The *device stream* is an unprocessed video stream. The *project stream* is the result of the processing done by the model on the video frames.

- Viewing a Device Stream
- Viewing a Project Stream
- Creating a Lambda Function for Viewing the Project Stream

Viewing a Device Stream

To view the unprocessed device stream

1. Plug your AWS DeepLens into a power outlet and turn it on.

2. Connect a USB mouse and keyboard to your AWS DeepLens.

3. Use the micro HDMI cable to connect your AWS DeepLens to a monitor. A login screen appears on the monitor.

4. Sign in to the device using the SSH password that you set when you registered the device.

5. To see the video stream from your AWS DeepLens, start your terminal and run the following command:

```
1 mplayer --demuxer lavf /opt/awscam/out/ch1_out.h264
```

6. To stop viewing the video stream and end your terminal session, press Ctrl+C.

Viewing a Project Stream

To view a project stream

1. Plug your AWS DeepLens to a power outlet and turn it on.

2. Connect a USB mouse and keyboard to your AWS DeepLens.

3. Use the micro HDMI cable to connect your AWS DeepLens to a monitor. A login screen appears on the monitor.

4. Sign in to the device using the SSH password you set when you registered the device.

5. To see the video stream from your AWS DeepLens, start your terminal and run the following command:

```
1 mplayer --demuxer lavf -lavfdopts format=mjpeg:probesize=32 /tmp/results.mjpeg
```

6. To stop viewing the video stream and end your terminal session, press Ctrl+C.

Creating a Lambda Function for Viewing the Project Stream

To view the project stream, you need an AWS Lambda function that interacts with the mjpeg stream on your device and the deep learning model. For the sample projects included with AWS DeepLens, the code is included in the inference Lambda function for the project. For your custom projects, you need to create a Lambda function that performs this task.

Create a Lambda function for your custom projects
Add the following sample code to your projects and change the model name and the dimensions as appropriate.

```
1  # -----------------------------------
2  # Copyright Amazon AWS DeepLens, 2017
3  # -----------------------------------
4
5  import os
6  import greengrasssdk
7  from threading import Timer
8  import time
9  import awscam
10 import cv2
11 from threading import Thread
12
13 # Creating a greengrass core sdk client
14 client = greengrasssdk.client('iot-data')
15
16 # The information exchanged between IoT and cloud has
17 # a topic and a message body.
18 # This is the topic that this code uses to send messages to cloud
19 iotTopic = '$aws/things/{}/infer'.format(os.environ['AWS_IOT_THING_NAME'])
20 ret, frame = awscam.getLastFrame()
21 ret,jpeg = cv2.imencode('.jpg', frame)
22 Write_To_FIFO = True
23 class FIFO_Thread(Thread):
24     def __init__(self):
25         ''' Constructor. '''
26         Thread.__init__(self)
27
28     def run(self):
29         fifo_path = "/tmp/results.mjpeg"
30         if not os.path.exists(fifo_path):
31             os.mkfifo(fifo_path)
32         f = open(fifo_path,'w')
33         client.publish(topic=iotTopic, payload="Opened Pipe")
34         while Write_To_FIFO:
35             try:
36                 f.write(jpeg.tobytes())
37             except IOError as e:
38                 continue
39
40 def greengrass_infinite_infer_run():
41     try:
42         modelPath = "/opt/awscam/artifacts/mxnet_deploy_ssd_resnet50_300_FP16_FUSED.xml"
43         modelType = "ssd"
44         input_width = 300
45         input_height = 300
46         max_threshold = 0.25
47         outMap = ({ 1: 'aeroplane', 2: 'bicycle', 3: 'bird', 4: 'boat',
48                     5: 'bottle', 6: 'bus', 7 : 'car', 8 : 'cat',
49                     9 : 'chair', 10 : 'cow', 11 : 'dinning table',
50                     12 : 'dog', 13 : 'horse', 14 : 'motorbike',
51                     15 : 'person', 16 : 'pottedplant', 17 : 'sheep',
52                     18 : 'sofa', 19 : 'train', 20 : 'tvmonitor' })
53         results_thread = FIFO_Thread()
54         results_thread.start()
```

```python
55
56         # Send a starting message to IoT console
57         client.publish(topic=iotTopic, payload="Object detection starts now")
58
59         # Load model to GPU (use {"GPU": 0} for CPU)
60         mcfg = {"GPU": 1}
61         model = awscam.Model(modelPath, mcfg)
62         client.publish(topic=iotTopic, payload="Model loaded")
63         ret, frame = awscam.getLastFrame()
64         if ret == False:
65             raise Exception("Failed to get frame from the stream")
66
67         yscale = float(frame.shape[0]/input_height)
68         xscale = float(frame.shape[1]/input_width)
69
70         doInfer = True
71         while doInfer:
72             # Get a frame from the video stream
73             ret, frame = awscam.getLastFrame()
74
75             # Raise an exception if failing to get a frame
76             if ret == False:
77                 raise Exception("Failed to get frame from the stream")
78
79             # Resize frame to fit model input requirement
80             frameResize = cv2.resize(frame, (input_width, input_height))
81
82             # Run model inference on the resized frame
83             inferOutput = model.doInference(frameResize)
84
85             # Output inference result to the fifo file so it can be viewed with mplayer
86             parsed_results = model.parseResult(modelType, inferOutput)['ssd']
87             label = '{'
88             for obj in parsed_results:
89                 if obj['prob'] > max_threshold:
90                     xmin = int( xscale * obj['xmin'] ) + int((obj['xmin'] - input_width/2) +
                            input_width/2)
91                     ymin = int( yscale * obj['ymin'] )
92                     xmax = int( xscale * obj['xmax'] ) + int((obj['xmax'] - input_width/2) +
                            input_width/2)
93                     ymax = int( yscale * obj['ymax'] )
94                     cv2.rectangle(frame, (xmin, ymin), (xmax, ymax), (255, 165, 20), 4)
95                     label += '"{}": {:.2f},'.format(outMap[obj['label']], obj['prob'] )
96                     label_show = "{}:    {:.2f}%".format(outMap[obj['label']], obj['prob']*100 )
97                     cv2.putText(frame, label_show, (xmin, ymin-15),cv2.FONT_HERSHEY_SIMPLEX,
                            0.5, (255, 165, 20), 4)
98             label += '"null": 0.0'
99             label += '}'
100            client.publish(topic=iotTopic, payload = label)
101            global jpeg
102            ret,jpeg = cv2.imencode('.jpg', frame)
103
104    except Exception as e:
105        msg = "Test failed: " + str(e)
```

22

```
106         client.publish(topic=iotTopic, payload=msg)
107
108     # Asynchronously schedule this function to be run again in 15 seconds
109     Timer(15, greengrass_infinite_infer_run).start()
110
111 # Execute the function above
112 greengrass_infinite_infer_run()
113
114 # This is a dummy handler and will not be invoked
115 # Instead the code above will be executed in an infinite loop for our example
116 def function_handler(event, context):
117     return
```

After you've created and deployed the Lambda function, see Viewing a Project Stream.

Working with AWS DeepLens Sample Projects

When your AWS DeepLens device is registered and connected, you can begin using it. To use your device for deep learning, you create a project and deploy it to your AWS DeepLens device. An AWS DeepLens *project* is made up of deep learning models and associated AWS Lambda functions.

AWS DeepLens comes with several sample projects that you can deploy and use right out of the box.

- AWS DeepLens Sample Projects Overview
- Creating and Deploying an AWS DeepLens Sample Project
- Extending any Project's Functionality
- Editing an Existing Model with Amazon SageMaker

AWS DeepLens Sample Projects Overview

To get started with AWS DeepLens, use the sample project templates. AWS DeepLens sample projects are projects where the model is pre-trained so that all you have to do is create the project, import the model, deploy the project, and run the project. Other sections in this guide teach you to extend a sample project's functionality so that it performs a specified task in response to an event, and train a sample project to do something different than the original sample.

Artistic Style Transfer

This project transfers the style of an image, such as a painting, to an entire video sequence captured by AWS DeepLens.

This project shows how a Convolutional Neural Network (CNN) can apply the style of a painting to your surroundings as it's streamed with your AWS DeepLens device. The project uses a pretrained optimized model that is ready to be deployed to your AWS DeepLens device. After deploying it, you can watch the stylized video stream.

You can also use your own image. After fine tuning the model for the image, you can watch as the CNN applies the image's style to your video stream.

- **Project model:** deeplens-artistic-style-transfer
- **Project function:** deeplens-artistic-style-transfer

Object Recognition

This project shows you how a deep learning model can detect and recognize objects in a room.

The project uses the Single Shot MultiBox Detector (SSD) framework to detect objects with a pretrained resnet_50 network. The network has been trained on the Pascal VOC dataset and is capable of recognizing 20 different kinds of objects. The model takes the video stream from your AWS DeepLens device as input and labels the objects that it identifies. The project uses a pretrained optimized model that is ready to be deployed to your AWS DeepLens device. After deploying it, you can watch your AWS DeepLens model recognize objects around you.

The model is able to recognize the following objects: airplane, bicycle, bird, boat, bottle, bus, car, cat, chair, cow, dining table, dog, horse, motorbike, person, potted plant, sheep, sofa, train, and TV monitor.

- **Project model:** deeplens-object-dectection
- **Project function:** deeplens-object-dectection

Face Detection and Recognition

With this project, you use a face detection model and your AWS DeepLens device to detect the faces of people in a room.

The model takes the video stream from your AWS DeepLens device as input and marks the images of faces that it detects. The project uses a pretrained optimized model that is ready to be deployed to your AWS DeepLens device.

- **Project model:** deeplens-face-detection
- **Project function:** deeplens-face-detection

Hot Dog Recognition

Inspired by a popular television show, this project classifies food as either a hot dog or not a hot dog.

It uses a model based on the SqueezeNet deep neural network. The model takes the video stream from your AWS DeepLens device as input, and labels images as a hot dog or not a hot dog. The project uses a pretrained, optimized model that is ready to be deployed to your AWS DeepLens device. After deploying the model, you can use the Live View feature to watch as the model recognizes hot dogs .

You can edit this model by creating Lambda functions that are triggered by the model's output. For example, if the model detects a hot dog, a Lambda function could send you an SMS message. To learn how to create this Lambda function, see Editing an Existing Model with Amazon SageMaker

Cat and Dog Recognition

This project shows how you can use deep learning to recognize a cat or a dog.

It is based on a convolutional neural network (CNN) architecture and uses a pretrained * Resnet-152* topology to classify an image as a cat or a dog. The project uses a pretrained, optimized model that is ready to be deployed to your AWS DeepLens device. After deploying it, you can watch as AWS DeepLens uses the model to recognize your pets.

- **Project model:** deeplens-cat-and-dog-recognition
- **Project function:** deeplens-cat-and-dog-recognition

Action Recognition

This project recognizes more than 30 kinds of activities.

It uses the Apache MXNet framework to transfer learning from a SqueezeNet trained with ImageNet to a new task. The network has been tuned on a subset of the UCF101 dataset and is capable of recognizing more than 30 different activities. The model takes the video stream from your AWS DeepLens device as input and labels the actions that it identifies. The project uses a pretrained, optimized model that is ready to be deployed to your AWS DeepLens device.

After deploying the model, you can watch your AWS DeepLens use the model to recognize 37 different activities, such as applying makeup, applying lipstick, participating in archery, playing basketball, bench pressing, biking, playing billiards, blowing drying your hair, blowing out candles, bowling, brushing teeth, cutting things in the kitchen, playing a drum, getting a haircut, hammering, handstand walking, getting a head massage, horseback riding, hula hooping, juggling, jumping rope, doing jumping jacks, doing lunges, using nunchucks, playing a cello, playing a flute, playing a guitar, playing a piano, playing a sitar, playing a violin, doing pushups, shaving, skiing, typing, walking a dog, writing on a board, and playing with a yo-yo.

- **Project model:** deeplens-action-recognition
- **Project function:** deeplens-action-recognition

Creating and Deploying an AWS DeepLens Sample Project

To help you get started with AWS DeepLens, we provide a number of sample AWS DeepLens project templates that you can use to create projects and get you up and going quickly. For more information, see AWS DeepLens Sample Projects Overview.

In this walkthrough, you create the Object Detection project. The Object Detection project analyzes images within a video stream on your AWS DeepLens device to identify objects. It can recognize as many as 20 types of objects.

Though the instructions here are specific to the Object Detection project, you can follow the same steps to create and deploy any of the sample projects. When creating a sample project, the fields in the console are pre-populated for you so you can accept the defaults. In the **Project content** portion of the screen, you need to know the project's model and function. That information is available for the individual projects in the AWS DeepLens Sample Projects Overview topic.

Your web browser is the interface between you and your AWS DeepLens device. You perform all of the following activities on the AWS DeepLens console using your browser.

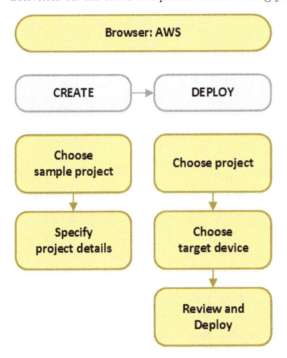

Step 1: Create Your Project

The following procedure creates the Object Detection sample project.

To create an AWS DeepLens project using a sample project

The steps for creating a project encompass two screens. On the first screen you select your project. On the second screen, you specify the project's details.

1. Using your browser, open the AWS DeepLens console at https://console.aws.amazon.com/deeplens/.

2. Choose **Projects**, then choose **Create new project**.

3. On the **Choose project type** screen

1. Choose **Use a project template**, then choose the sample project you want to create. For this exercise, choose **Object detection**.

2. Scroll to the bottom of the screen, then choose **Next**.

4. On the **Specify project details** screen

   1. In the **Project information** section:

      1. Either accept the default name for the project, or type a name you prefer.

      2. Either accept the default description for the project, or type a description you prefer.

   2. In the **Project content** section:

      1. **Model**—make sure the model is the correct model for the project you're creating. For this exercise it should be *deeplens-object-detection*. If it isn't, remove the current model then choose **Add model**. From the list of models, choose *deeplens-object-detection*.

      2. **Function**—make sure the functiion is the correct function for the project you're creating. For this exercise it should be *deeplens-object-detection*. If it isn't, remove the current function then choose **Add function**. From the list of functions, choose *deeplens-object-detection*.

   3. Choose **Create**.

      This returns you to the **Projects** screen where the project you just created is listed with your other projects.

Step 2: Deploy Your Project

In this walkthrough, you deploy the Object Detection project.

Your web browser is the interface between you and your AWS DeepLens device. You perform all of the following activities on your browser after logging on to AWS:

1. On the **Projects** screen, choose the radio button to the left of your project name, then choose **Deploy to device**.

2. On the **Target device** screen, from the list of AWS DeepLens devices, choose the radio button to the left of the device that you want to deploy this project to. An AWS DeepLens device can have only one project deployed to it at a time.

3. Choose **Review**.

   If a project is already deployed to the device, you will see an error message that deploying this project will overwrite the project that is already running on the device. Choose **Continue project**.

   This will take you to the **Review and deploy** screen.

4. On the **Review and deploy** screen, review your project and choose either **Previous** to go back and make changes, or **Deploy** to deploy the project. **Important**
   Deploying a project incurs costs for the AWS services that are used to run the project.

For instructions on viewing your project's output, see Viewing AWS DeepLens Project Output.

Extending any Project's Functionality

In this section, you take the "Hotdog recognition" sample project and add some rule-based functionality to it to make AWS DeepLens send an SMS notification whenever it detects a hot dog. Though we use the "Hotdog recognition" sample project in this topic, this process could be used for any project, sample or custom.

This section demonstrates how to extend your AWS DeepLens projects to interact with other AWS services. For example, you could extend AWS DeepLens to create:

- A dashboard and search interface for all objects and faces detected by AWS DeepLens with timelines and frames using Amazon Elasticsearch Service.

- Anomaly detection models to detect the number of people walking in front of your store using Kinesis Data Analytics.

- A face detection and celebrity recognition application to identity VIPs around you using Amazon Rekognition.

In this exercise, you modify the project you previously created and edited (see Editing an Existing Model with Amazon SageMaker) to use the AWS IoT rules engine and an AWS Lambda function.

- Create and Configure the Lambda Function
  - Create a Lambda Function
  - Add an AWS IoT Rule
  - Configure the Lambda Function
  - Test Your Configuration
  - Test Using the Hot Dog Project
- Disable the AWS IoT Rule

Create and Configure the Lambda Function

Create and configure an AWS Lambda function that runs in the Cloud and filters the messages from your AWS DeepLens device for those that have a high enough probability (>0.5) of being a hot dog. You can also change the probability threshold.

Create a Lambda Function

1. Sign in to the AWS Management Console and open the AWS Lambda console at https://console.aws. amazon.com/lambda/.

   Make sure you have selected the US East (N. Virginia) AWS Region.

2. Choose **Create function**.

3. Place your cursor in the **Blueprints** box, then choose **Blueprint name**. When **Blueprint name:** appears, type and choose **iot-button-email**.

4. Choose **Author from scratch**.

5. Type a name for the Lambda function, for example, **_hotdog_notifier**.

6. For **Role**, keep **Create a new Role from template(s)**.

7. Type a name for the role; for example, **_hotdog_notifier**.

8. For **Policy Templates**, choose **SNS Publish policy**.

9. Choose **Create function**.

Add an AWS IoT Rule

This AWS IoT rule specifies the source of the data that triggers the action you specify in your Lambda function (the next step).

1. Scroll down to **aws-iot**.

2. For **IoT type**, choose **Custom IoT rule**.

3. For **Rule**, choose **Create new rule**.

4. Type a name (*<your-name>_search_hotdogs*) and a description for the rule.

5. Paste the following into the **Rule query statement** box. Replace the red text with the AWS IoT topic for your AWS DeepLens. To find the AWS IoT topic, navigate to **Devices** on your AWS DeepLens, choose your device, then scroll to the bottom of the device detail page.

```
1 Select Hotdog from '/$aws/deeplens/KJHFD-DKJO87-LJLKD/inference'
```

This query captures messages from your AWS DeepLens in JSON format:

```
1 { "Hotdog" : "0.5438" }
```

6. Choose **Enable trigger**.

7. Scroll to the bottom of the page and choose **Create function**.

Configure the Lambda Function

Configure the Lambda function by replacing the default code with custom code and adding an environmental variable. For this project, you also need to modify the custom code that we provide.

1. In AWS Lambda, choose **Functions**, then choose the name of your function.

2. On the *your-name_hotdog_notifier* page, choose **Configuration**.

3. In the function code box, delete all of the code.

4. Paste the following code in the function code box. You need to change one line in the code to indicate how you want to get notifications. You do that in the next step.

```
1 /**
2  * This is a sample Lambda function that sends an SMS notification when your
3  * AWS DeepLens device detects a hot dog.
4  *
5  * Follow these steps to complete the configuration of your function:
6  *
7  * Update the phone number environment variable with your phone number.
8  */
9
10 const AWS = require('aws-sdk');
11
12 /**
13  * Replace the next line of code with one of the lines of code from the list following this
         code block.
14  */
15 const var=process.env.var;
16 const SNS = new AWS.SNS({ apiVersion: '2010-03-31' });
17
18 exports.handler = (event, context, callback) => {
```

```
19 console.log('Received event:', event);
20
21 // publish message
22 const params = {
23 Message: 'Your AWS DeepLens device just identified a hot dog. Congratulations!',
24 PhoneNumber: phone_number
25 };
26 if (event.label.includes("Hotdog")
27 SNS.publish(params, callback);
28 };
```

5. Add one of the following lines of code in the location indicated in the code block. In the next step, you add an environmental variable that corresponds to the code change you make here.

   - To receive email notifications: **const email=process.env.email;**

   - To receive phone notifications: **const phone_number=process.env.phone_number;**

6. Choose **Environmental variables** and add one of the following:
   [See the AWS documentation website for more details]

   The key value must match the `const` name in the line of code that you added in the previous step.

7. Choose **Save and test** (on the upper right).

Test Your Configuration

To test your configuration

1. Navigate to the AWS IoT console at https://console.aws.amazon.com/iot.

2. Choose **Test**.

3. Publish the following message to the topic that you defined in your rule: { "Hotdog" : "0.6382" }.

   You should receive the SMS message that you defined in your Lambda function: Your AWS DeepLens device just identified a hot dog. Congratulations!

Test Using the Hot Dog Project

If you haven't already deployed the Hot Dog project, do the following.

1. Navigate to https://console.aws.amazon.com/deeplens/home?region=us-east-1#firstrun/ and choose **Projects/Create a project template/Hotdog or Not Hotdog**.

2. Deploy the project to your device.

   For more information, see Creating and Deploying an AWS DeepLens Sample Project.

3. Show your AWS DeepLens a hot dog to see if it detects it and sends you the confirmation message.

To experiment, change the probability threshold for triggering the Lambda function and see what happens.

Disable the AWS IoT Rule

Unless you want AWS DeepLens to keep notifying you when it sees a hot dog, disable the AWS IoT rule.

1. Log in to the AWS IoT console at "https://console.aws.amazon.com/iot.

2. Choose **Act**, then choose the rule that you created for this exercise, *<your-name>*_**search_hotdogs**.

3. In the upper-right corner, choose **Actions**, then choose **Disable**.

Editing an Existing Model with Amazon SageMaker

In this example, you start with a SqueezeNet object detection model and use Amazon SageMaker to train it to perform binary classification to determine whether an object is a hot dog. The example shows you how to edit a model to perform binary classification, and explains learning rate and epochs. We have provided a Jupyter notebook instance, which is open source software for interactive computing. It includes the editing code to execute and explanations for the entire process.

After training the model, you import its artifacts into AWS DeepLens, and create a project. You then watch as your AWS DeepLens detects and identifies hot dogs.

- Step 1: Create an Amazon S3 Bucket
- Step 2: Create an Amazon SageMaker Notebook Instance
- Step 3: Edit the Model in Amazon SageMaker
- Step 4: Optimize the Model
- Step 5: Import the Model
- Step 6: Create an Inference Lambda Function
- Step 7: Create a New AWS DeepLens Project
- Step 8: Review and Deploy the Project
- Step 9: View Your Model's Output

Step 1: Create an Amazon S3 Bucket

Before you begin, be sure that you have created an AWS account, and the required IAM users and roles.

1. Sign in to the AWS Management Console and open the Amazon S3 console at https://console.aws.amazon.com/s3/.

   Make sure you are in the US East (N. Virginia) region.

2. Choose **Create bucket**.

3. On the **Name and region** screen:

   1. Name the bucket **deeplens-sagemaker-<*your-name*>**. The bucket name must begin with **deeplens-sagemaker-** or the services will not be able to access it.

   2. Verify that you are in the US East (N. Virginia) region.

   3. Choose **Next**.

4. On the **Set properties** screen choose **Next**.

5. On the **Set permissions** screen, verify that both **Objects** and **Object permissions** have both the *Read* and *Write* permissions set, then choose **Next**.

6. On the **Review** screen, review your settings then choose **Create bucket** which creates your Amazon S3 bucket and returns you to the Amazon S3 screen.

7. On the Amazon S3 screen, locate and choose your bucket's name.

8. On your bucket's screen, choose **Permissions**, then under **Public access** choose *Everyone*.

9. On the **Everyone** popup, under **Access to objects** enable *List objects* and *Write objects*. Under **Access to this bucket's ACL** enable *Read bucket permissions* and *Write bucket permissions*, then choose **Save**.

10. After you return to your bucket's page, choose **Overview** then choose **Create folder**.

11. Name the folder *test* then choose **Save**.

Step 2: Create an Amazon SageMaker Notebook Instance

Create an Amazon SageMaker notebook instance.

1. Open the Amazon SageMaker console at https://console.aws.amazon.com/sagemaker/.

   Make sure that you have chosen the us-east-1 — US East (N. Virginia) Region.

2. Choose **Create notebook instance**.

3. On the **Create notebook instance** page, then do the following:

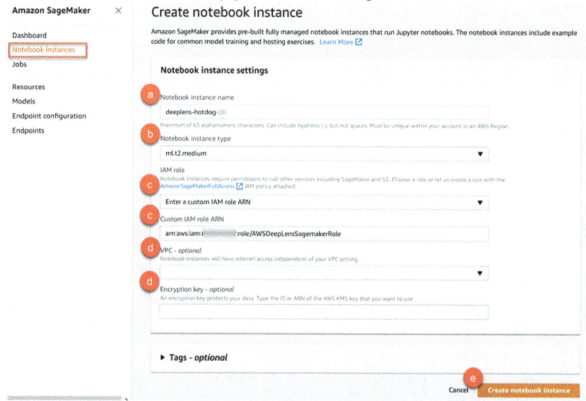

1. For **Notebook instance name**, type a name; for example, *<your-name>*-hotdog.

2. For **Instance type**, choose ml.t2.medium.

3. For **IAM role ** choose **Enter a custom IAM role ARN**, paste the Amazon Resource Name (ARN) of your Amazon SageMaker role in the **Custom IAM role ARN** box.

   To find the ARN of your Amazon SageMaker role:

   1. Open the IAM console at https://console.aws.amazon.com/iam/.

   2. In the navigation pane, choose **Roles**.

   3. Find the **AWSDeepLensSagemakerRole** and choose its name. This takes you to the role's **Summary** page.

   4. On the **Summary** page, locate and copy the **Role ARN**. The ARN will look something like this:

```
1  arn:aws:iam::account id:role/AWSDeepLensSagemakerRole
```

4. Both **VPC** and **Encryption key** are optional. Skip them. **Tip**
   If you want to access resources in your VPC from the notebook instance, choose a **VPC** and a

SubnetId. For **Security Group**, choose the default security group of the VPC. The inbound and outbound rules of the default security group are sufficient for the exercises in this guide.

5. Choose **Create notebookinstance**.

Your new notebook instance is now available on the **Notebooks** page.

Step 3: Edit the Model in Amazon SageMaker

In this step, you open the *<your-name>*-hotdog notebook and edit the object detection model so it recognizes a hot dog. The notebook contains explanations to help you through each step.

1. Open the Amazon SageMaker console at https://console.aws.amazon.com/sagemaker/.

2. Choose the US East (N. Virginia) Region is chosen.

3. In the navigation pane, choose **Notebook instances**.

4. On the **Notebooks** page, choose the radio button to the left of the notebook instance that you just created (*<your-name>*-hotdog). When the notebook's status is *InService*, choose **Open**.

5. Open a new tab in your browser and navigate to https://github.com/aws-samples/reinvent-2017-deeplens-workshop.

6. Download the .zip file or clone the Git repository with the following command. If you downloaded the .zip file, locate it and extract all.

```
1  git clone git@github.com:aws-samples/reinvent-2017-deeplens-workshop.git
```

If you downloaded the .zip file, locate it and extract all.

You now upload the training file and use it to edit the model.

1. On the Jupyter tab, choose **Upload**.

2. Navigate to the extracted file `deeplens-hotdog-or-not-hotdog.ipynb` then choose **Open**, then choose **Upload**.

3. Locate and choose the *deeplens-hotdog-or-not-hotdog* notebook.

4. In the upper right corner of the Jupyter screen, verify that the kernal is `conda_mxnet_p36`. If it isn't, change the kernal.

5. In the `deeplens-hotdog-or-not-hotdog.ipynb` file, search for **bucket=** *'your S3 bucket name here'*. Replace *'your s3 bucket name here'* with the name of your S3 bucket, for example **deeplens-sagemaker-<your-name>**.

Return to the top of the file.

For each step (`In [#]:`) in the file:

1. Read the step's description.

2. If the block has code in it, place your cursor in the code block and run the code block. To run a code block in Jupyter, use **Ctrl+** (macOS **Cnd_**) or choose the run icon (▶). **Important**
   Each step is numbered in a fashion such as `In [1]:`. While the block is executing, that changes to `In [*]:`. When the block finishes executing it returns to `In [1]:`. Do not move on to the next code block while the current block is still running.

6. After you finish editing the model, return to the Amazon S3 console, choose your bucket name, choose the `test` folder, and then verify that the following artifacts of the edited model are stored in your S3 bucket's test folder.

   - Hotdog_or_not_model-0000.params

- Hotdog_or_not_model-symbol.json

Step 4: Optimize the Model

Now that you have a trained mxNet model there is one final step that is required before you run the model on the AWS DeepLens's GPU. The trained mxNet model does not come in a computationally optimized format. If we deploy the model in the original format it will run on the CPU via mxNet at sub optimal speed. In order to run the model at optimal speed on the GPU we need to perform model optimization. For instructions on how to optimize your MXNet model, see Optimizing a Custom Model.

Step 5: Import the Model

Import the edited model into AWS DeepLens.

1. Using your browser, open the AWS DeepLens console at https://console.aws.amazon.com/deeplens/.
2. Choose **Models**, then choose **Import model**.
3. For **Import model to AWS DeepLens**, choose **Externally trained model**.
4. For **Model settings**, do the following:
    1. For **Model artifact**, type the path to the artifacts that you uploaded to the Amazon S3 bucket in the previous step. The path begins with **s3://deeplens-**. For example, if you followed the naming in Step 1, the path will be **s3://deeplens-sagemaker-*<your-name>*/**.
    2. For **Model name**, type a name for the model.
    3. For **Model description**, type a description.
5. Choose **Import model**.

Step 6: Create an Inference Lambda Function

Use the AWS Lambda console to create a Lambda function that uses your model. For specific instructions with sample code, see Creating an AWS DeepLens Inference Lambda Function.

Step 7: Create a New AWS DeepLens Project

Now create a new AWS DeepLens project and add the edited model to it.

1. Using your browser, open the AWS DeepLens console at https://console.aws.amazon.com/deeplens/.
2. Choose **Projects**.
3. Choose **Create new project**.
4. For **Choose project type**, choose **Create a new blank project**, then choose **Next**.
5. For **Project information**, type a name and description for this project.
6. For **Project content**, choose **Add model**.
7. Search for and choose the model that you just created, then choose **Add model**.
8. Choose **Add function**, then choose **deeplens-hotdog-o-hotdog**, then choose **Add function**.
9. Choose **Create**.

Step 8: Review and Deploy the Project

1. Using your browser, open the AWS DeepLens console at https://console.aws.amazon.com/deeplens/.

2. From the list of projects, choose the project that you just created, then choose **Deploy to device**.

3. Choose your AWS DeepLens as your target device, then choose **Review**.

4. Review the settings, then choose **Deploy**. **Important**
   Deploying a project incurs costs for the various AWS services that are used.

Step 9: View Your Model's Output

To view your model's output, follow the instructions at Viewing AWS DeepLens Project Output.

Working with AWS DeepLens Custom Projects

When you are ready, you can create and deploy your own projects. The topics in this section cover the tasks you need to perform to create, optimize, and deploy your personal projects.

- Importing Your Amazon SageMaker Trained Model
- Importing an Externally Trained Model
- Optimizing a Custom Model
- Creating an AWS DeepLens Inference Lambda Function

Importing Your Amazon SageMaker Trained Model

To use your Amazon SageMaker trained module you must import it into AWS DeepLens.

To import your Amazon SageMaker trained model into AWS DeepLens

1. Open the AWS DeepLens console at https://console.aws.amazon.com/deeplens/.

2. From the navigation pane, choose **Models** then choose **Import model**.

3. For **Import source** choose **Amazon SageMaker trained model**.

4. In the **Model settings** area:

    1. From the list of completed jobs, choose the **Amazon SageMaker training job ID** for the model you want to import.

       The ID of the job must begin with `deeplens-`. If you do not find the job you're looking for in the list, go to the Amazon SageMaker console and check the status of the jobs to verify that it has successfully completed.

    2. For the **Model name**, type the name you want for the model. Model names can contain alphanumeric characters and hypens, and be no longer than 100 characters.

    3. For the **Description** you can optionally type in a description for your model.

    4. Choose **Import model**.

Importing an Externally Trained Model

To use an externally trained model, import it.

To import an externally trained model

1. Sign in to the AWS Management Console and open the AWS DeepLens console at https://console.aws. amazon.com/deeplens/.

2. In the navigation pane, choose **Models**, then choose **Import model**.

3. into For **Import source**, choose **Externally trained model**.

4. For **Model settings**, provide the following information.

   1. For **Model artifact path**, type the full path to the Amazon Simple Storage Service (Amazon S3) location of the artifacts created when you trained your model. The path begins with **s3://deeplens-**. For example, if you followed the naming conventions we use throughout this documentation, the path will be **s3://deeplens-sagemaker-*your_name*/**.

   2. For **Model name**, type a name. A model name can have a maximum of 100 alphanumeric characters and hypens.

   3. Optional. For **Description**, type a description of the model.

   4. Choose **Import model**.

Optimizing a Custom Model

To access the GPU for inference, AWS DeepLens uses the clDNN, Compute Library for Deep Neural Networks. To run your own models on AWS DeepLens, you have to convert them into clDNN format. The model optimizer converts the format with the following code:

```
1 error, model_path = mo.optimize(model_name,input_width,input_height)
```

You include the model optimizer code in an inference Lambda function, which is required to allow AWS DeepLens to access deployed models.

For information on how to create an inference Lambda function that includes the model optimizer, see Creating an AWS DeepLens Inference Lambda Function.

For more information about the model optimizer, see AWS DeepLens Model Optimzer API.

Creating an AWS DeepLens Inference Lambda Function

In this topic, you create an inference Lambda function that performs three key functions: preprocessing, inference, and postprocessing. Each step is accompanied by the associated code. For the complete function code, see The Completed Lambda Function.

To create an AWS DeepLens inference Lambda function

1. Sign in to the AWS Management Console and open the AWS Lambda console at https://console.aws. amazon.com/lambda/.

2. Choose **Create function**, then choose **Blueprints**.

3. Choose the **Blueprints** box then from the dropdown, choose **Blueprint name** and type **greengrass-hello-world**.

4. When the *greengrass-hello-world* blueprint appears, choose it, then choose **Configure**.

5. In the **Basic information** section:

    1. Type a name for your Lambda function.

    2. From the **Role** list, choose **Choose an existing role**.

    3. Choose **AWSDeepLensLambdaRole**, which you created when you registered your device.

6. Scroll to the bottom of the page and choose **Create function**.

7. In the function code box, makes sure that the handler is `greengrassHelloWorld.function_handler`. The name of the function handler must match the name of the Python script that you want to run. In this case, you are running the `greengrassHelloWorld.py` script, so the name of the function handler is `greengrassHelloWorld.function_handler`.

8. Delete all of the code in the `GreengrassHelloWorld.py` box and replace it with the code that you generate in the rest of this procedure.

9. Add the following code to your Lambda function.

    1. Import these required packages:

        - `os`—Allows your Lambda function to access the AWS DeepLens operating system.

        - `awscam`—Allows your Lambda function to use the AWS DeepLens Device Library. For more information, see Model.

        - `mo` — Allows your Lambda function to access the AWS DeepLens model optimizer. For more information, see AWS DeepLens Model Optimzer API.

        - `cv2`—Allows your Lambda function to access the Open CV library, which contains tools for image preprocessing.

        - `thread`—Allows your Lambda function to access Python's multi-threading library.

        To import these packages, copy and paste the following code into the `GreengrassHello` file.

        ```
        1 import os
        2 import awscam
        3 import mo
        4 import cv2
        5 from threading import Thread
        ```

    2. Create a Greengrass SDK client. You will use this client to send messages to the cloud.

        ```
        1 client = greengrasssdk.client('iot-data')
        ```

3. Create an AWS IoT topic for your Lambda function's messages. You can access this topic in the AWS IoT console.

```
1 iot_topic = '$aws/things/{}/infer'.format(os.environ['AWS_IOT_THING_NAME'])
```

4. To view the output locally with mplayer, declare a global variable that contains the .jpeg image that you send to the FIFO file `results.mjpeg`.

```
1 jpeg = None
2 Write_To_FIFO = True
3 # making Write_To_FIFO = False kills the thread so you cannot view your output over
    mplayer
```

5. To publish the output images to the FIFO file and view them with mplayer, create a class that runs on its own thread.

```
1 class FIFO_Thread(Thread):
2         def __init__(self):
3             '''Constructor.'''
4             Thread.__init__(self)
5
6         def run(self):
7             fifo_path = "/tmp/results.mjpeg"
8             if not os.path.exists(fifo_path):
9                 os.mkfifo(fifo_path)
10            f = open(fifo_path,'w')
11            client.publish(topic=iot_topic, payload="Opened Pipe")
12
13            while Write_To_FIFO
14               try:
15                   f.write(jpeg.tobytes())
16               except IOError as e:
17                   continue
```

6. Define an inference class.

   1. Define an AWS Greengrass inference function. `input_width` and `input_height` define the width and height of the input in pixels. To perform inference, the model expects frames of this size. You can customize these values for the model that you are deploying to AWS DeepLens.

   ```
   1 def greengrass_infinite_infer_run():
   2 input_width  = 224
   3 input_height = 224
   ```

   2. Name the model. The name is the prefix of the trained model's `params` and `json` files. For example, if the files are named `squeezenet_v1.1-0000.params` and `squeezenet_v1.1-0000.json`, the model name is the prefix `squeezenet_v1.1`. **Important**
   The model name must match the prefix. Otherwise, the model can't perform inference, and generates an error.

   ```
   1 model_name = 'squeezenet_v1'
   ```

   3. Initialize the model optimizer. The model optimizer converts the deployed model to clDNN format, which is accessible to the AWS DeepLens GPU. The model optimizer returns the path to the post-optimized artifacts.

   ```
   1 error, model_path = mo.optimize(model_name, input_width, input_height)
   ```

4. Load the model into the inference engine. To use the CPU, instead of the GPU, specify `"GPU":0`. The CPU is much less efficient, so we don't recommend using it.

```
1 model = awscam.Model(model_path,{"GPU":1})
2 # You can send a message to AWS IoT to show that the model is loaded.
3 client.publish(topic=iot_topic, payload="Model loaded.")
```

5. Define the type of model that you are running. The options are:

   - `segmentation`—For neural style transfer.
   - `ssd`—Single shot detector. For object localization it includes a definition of the locale in the frame that the object occupies by drawing a bounding box around the object.
   - `classification`—For image classification.

   Because you are deploying a SqueezeNet model that classifies images, define the model type as `classification`.

```
1 model_type = "classification"
```

6. Map the numeric label generated by the model to a human-readable label. Because squeezenet_v1.1 has 1,000 classifiers, it's unrealistic to create the mapping in code. Instead, add a text file to the Lambda .zip file. You can then load the labels into a list where the index of the list represents the label returned by the network.

```
1 with open('sysnet.txt', 'r') as f:
2    labels = [l.rstrip() for l in f]
```

7. Define the number of classifiers that you want to see in the output.

```
1 topk = 5
```

   The value 5 specifies that the top 5 values with the highest probability are output, in descending order. You can specify any value as long as it's supported by the model.

8. Start the FIFO thread so you can view the output with the mplayer.

```
1 results_thread = FIFO_Thread()
2    results_thread.start()
3    # You can publish an "Inference starting" message to the AWS IoT console.
4    client.publish(topic = iot_topic, payload = "Inference starting")
```

9. Get the most recent frame from the AWS DeepLens camera. If the latest frame is not returned, raise an exception.

```
1 ret, frame = awscam.getLastFrame()
2 if ret == False:
3   raise Exception("Failed to get frame from the stream")
```

10. Preprocess the input frame from the camera by making sure that its dimensions match the dimensions of the frame that the model was trained on. To resize the input frame, specify the input dimensions defined earlier, `input_width` and `input_height`. Depending on the model that you trained, you might need to perform other preprocessing steps, such as image normalization.

```
1 frame_resize = cv2.resize(frame, (input_width, input_height))
```

11. Perform inference on the resized frame.

```
1 infer_output = mdel.doInference(frame_resize)
```

12. Parse the results.

```
1 parsed_results = model.parseResult(model_type, infer_output)
```

13. Display only the n results that have the highest probability.

```
1 top_k = parsed_results[model_type][0:topk]
```

14. Send the results to the cloud.

First, put the message in JSON format. This allows other Lambda functions in the cloud to subscribe to the AWS IoT topic and perform actions when they detect an interesting event.

```
1 msg = "{"
2   prob_num = 0
3   for obj in top_k
4     if prob_num == topk-1:
5       msg += '"{}":{:.2f}'.format(labels[obj["label"]],obj["prob"])
6     else:
7       msg += '"{}":{:.2f},'.format(labels[obj["label"]], obj["prob"])
8     prob_num += 1
9   msg += "}"
```

Then send it to the cloud.

```
1 client.publish(topic="iot_topic, payload = msg)
```

15. Postprocess the image. In this case add a line of text to the image: a label of the most likely results.

```
1 cv2.putText(frame, labels[top_k[0]["label"]], (0,22), cv2.FONT_HERSHEY_SIMPLEX, 1,
    (255, 165, 20), 4)
```

16. Update the global jpeg variable so you can view the results with mplayer.

```
1 global jpeg
2 ret, jpeg = cv2.imencode('.jpg', frame)
3 # If you want, you can add exception handling as follows.
4 # '   Dont forget to put the preceding code in a try block.
5 except Exception as e:
6   msg = "Lambda function failed: " + str(e)
7   client.publish(topic=iot_topic, payload = msg)
```

17. Run the function and view the results.

```
1 greengrass_infinite_infer_run()
```

Make sure that you save and publish the function code. If you don't, you can't view the inference Lambda function that you just created in the AWS DeepLens console.

For questions or help, see the AWS DeepLens forum at Forum: AWS DeepLens.

The Completed Lambda Function

The following code creates the Lambda function that allows AWS DeepLens to access deployed models.

```
 1 # ------------------------------------
 2 # Copyright Amazon AWS DeepLens, ©2018
 3 # ------------------------------------
 4 import os                        # access to operating system for AWS DeepLens
 5 import awscam                    # access to AWS DeepLens Device Library
 6 import mo                        # access to AWS DeepLens model optimizer
 7 import cv2                       # access to Open CV library
 8 from threading import Thread     # access to Python's multi-threading library
 9
10 # create a Greengrasscore SDK client
11 client = greengrasssdk.client('iot-data')
12
13 # create AWS IoT for the Lambda function to send messages
14 iot_topic = '$aws/things/{}/infer'.format(os.environ['AWS_IOT_THING_NAME'])
15
16 # global variable to contain jpeg image
17 jpeg = None
18 Write_To_FIFO = True
19 # making Write_To_FIFO = False kills the thread so you cannot view your output over mplayer
20
21 # create a simple class that runs on its own thread so we can publish output images
22 #     to the FIFO file and view using mplayer
23 class FIFO_Thread(Thread):
24     def __init__(self):
25         '''Constructor.'''
26         Thread.__init__(self)
27
28     def run(self):
29         fifo_path = "/tmp/results.mjpeg"
30         if not os.path.exists(fifo_path):
31             os.mkfifo(fifo_path)
32         f = open(fifo_path,'w')
33         client.publish(topic=iot_topic, payload="Opened Pipe")
34
35         while Write_To_FIFO
36             try:
37                 f.write(jpeg.tobytes())
38             except IOError as e:
39                 continue
40
41 # define inference class within the Lambda function
42 def greengrass_infinite_infer_run():
43     input_width  = 224
44     input_height = 224
45
46     # define the name of he model
47     model_name = 'squeezenet_v1'
48
49 # optimize the model into Cl-DNN format
50 error, model_path = mo.optimize(model_name, input_width, input_height)
51
52 # load the model into the inference engine
53 model = awscam.Model(model_path,{"GPU":1})
54 # You can send a message to AWS IoT to show that the model is loaded.
```

```
55  client.publish(topic=iot_topic, payload="Model loaded.")
56
57  # define the type of model
58  #    possibilities are:
59  #        segmentation - for neural style transfers
60  #        ssd - (single shot detector) for object localization
61  #        classification - for image classification
62  model_type = "classification"
63
64  # load the labels into a list where the index represents the label returned by the network
65  with open('sysnet.txt', 'r') as f:
66      labels = [l.rstrip() for l in f]
67
68  # define the number of classifiers to see
69  topk = 5
70
71  # start the FIFO thread to view the output locally
72  results_thread = FIFO_Thread()
73      results_thread.start()
74      # you can publish an "Inference starting" message to the AWS IoT console
75      client.publish(topic = iot_topic, payload = "Inference starting")
76
77  # access the latest frame on the mjpeg stream
78  ret, frame = awscam.getLastFrame()
79  if ret == False:
80      raise Exception("Failed to get frame from the stream")
81
82  # resize the frame to the size expected by the model
83  frame_resize = cv2.resize(frame, (input_width, input_height))
84
85  # do inference on the frame
86  infer_output = mdel.doInference(frame_resize)
87
88  # parse the results and keep the top topk results
89  parsed_results = model.parseResult(model_type, infer_output)
90  top_k = parsed_results[model_type][0:topk]
91
92  # format the results as JSON and send to the cloud
93  msg = "{"
94      prob_num = 0
95      for obj in top_k:
96          if prob_num == topk-1:
97              msg += '"{}":{:.2f}'.format(labels[obj["label"]],obj["prob"])
98          else:
99              msg += '"{}":{:.2f},'.format(labels[obj["label"]], obj["prob"])
100         prob_num += 1
101     msg += "}"
102 client.publish(topic = iot_topic, payload = msg)
103
104 # post-process the image to view it on the mplayer
105 #    add a line of text to the image: a label of the most likely results
106 cv2.putText(frame, labels[top_k[0]["label"]], (0,22), cv2.FONT_HERSHEY_SIMPLEX, 1, (255, 165,
        20), 4)
107
```

```
108 # define a global variable so results can be viewed using mplayer
109 global jpeg
110 ret, jpeg = cv2.imencode('.jpg', frame)
111 # Catch an exception in case something went wrong
112 except Exception as e:
113     msg = "Lambda function failed: " + str(e)
114     client.publish(topic=iot_topic, payload = msg)
115
116 # run the function and view the results
117 greengrass_infinite_infer_run()
```

Managing Your AWS DeepLens Device

The following topics explain how to manage your AWS DeepLens device:

- Updating Your AWS DeepLens Device
- Deregister an AWS DeepLens Device

Updating Your AWS DeepLens Device

When you set up your device, you had the option to enable automatic updates (see Step 3:iii in Set Up Your AWS DeepLens Device). If you enabled automatic updates, you don't need to do anything more to update the software on your device. If you didn't enable automatic updates, you need to manually update your device periodically.

To manually update your AWS DeepLens using your password

1. Plug in your AWS DeepLens and turn it on.

2. Use a micro HDMI cable to connect your AWS DeepLens to a monitor.

3. Connect a USB mouse and keyboard to your AWS DeepLens.

4. When the login screen appears, sign in to the device using the SSH password you set when you registered it.

5. Start your terminal and run each of the following commands:

```
1 sudo apt-get update
2 sudo apt-get install awscam
3 sudo reboot
```

To manually update your AWS DeepLens using your IP address

1. Find your IP address by either logging into Ubuntu. or looking at your Wi-Fi router.

2. Start a terminal and type:

```
1 ssh aws_cam@IP-address
```

3. Run each of the following commands:

```
1 sudo apt-get update
2 sudo apt-get install awscam
3 sudo reboot
```

Deregister an AWS DeepLens Device

Deregistering your AWS DeepLens disassociates your AWS account and credentials from the device. Before you deregister your device, delete the photos or videos that are stored on it.

To deregister your AWS DeepLens

1. Open the AWS DeepLens console at https://console.aws.amazon.com/deeplens/home?region=us-east-1#firstrun/.

2. Remove all projects associated with the device.

   1. Choose **Devices**, then choose the radio button of the device that you want to deregister.

   2. In **Projects**, choose **Remove projects. Important**
      Delete the photos or videos that are stored on the device, using SSH and the SSH password that you set when you registered the device to log on to the device. Navigate to the folder where the photos or videos are stored and delete them.

3. Deregister the device.

   1. Choose **Devices**.

   2. Choose the name of the device you want to deregister, then choose **Deregister**.

   3. When the warning appears, choose **Deregister**.

Your AWS DeepLens is now deregistered. To use it again, repeat each of these steps:

- Register Your AWS DeepLens Device
- Connect AWS DeepLens to the Network
- Set Up Your AWS DeepLens Device
- Verify That Your AWS DeepLens Is Connected

AWS DeepLens Model Optimzer API

Custom models run inefficiently on the CPU. To run a custom model efficiently on the GPU, use the AWS DeepLens model optimizer API. The model optimizer class has a single method, `mo.optimize`, which optimizes your model to Cl-DNN format so it can run on the GPU.

```
1 class mo
```

Represents an AWS DeepLens model optimizer.

- Method mo.optimize()

AWS DeepLens Device Library

The AWS DeepLens Python device library provides classes and methods for the following:

- Running your inference code on your AWS DeepLens device. You can use these classes and methods in Lambda functions in your inference Lambda code.

- Model
  - Constructor
  - model.doInference(video_frame)
  - model.parseResult(model_type, raw_infer_result)

- Method awscam.getLastFrame()

Model

`class awscam.Model`

Represents an AWS DeepLens machine learning model.

```
1 import awscam
2 model = awscam.Model(model_topology_file, loading_config)
```

- Constructor
- model.doInference(video_frame)
- model.parseResult(model_type, raw_infer_result)

Constructor

The constructor for a `awscam.Model`

Request Syntax

```
1 import awscam
2 model = awscam.Model(model_topology_file, loading_config)
```

Parameters

- `model_topology_file`—Required. A neural network topology file (.xml) from the Intel model optimizer.

  Models supported: Classification and Single Shot MultiBox Detector (SSD)

- `loading_config` (dict)—Required. Specifies whether the model should be loaded into the GPU or CPU. The format of this parameter is a dictionary.

Permitted values:

- `{"GPU":1}`—Loads the model into the GPU
- `{"GPU":0}`—Loads the model into the CPU

model.doInference(video_frame)

Runs inference on a video frame (image file) by applying the loaded model. The method returns the result of the inference.

Request Syntax

```
1 import awscam
2 model = awscam.Model(model_topology_file, loading_config)
3 result = model.doInference(video_frame)
```

Parameters

- `video_frame`—Required. The model runs its inference on a video frame (image file) and returns the result of the model inference, which is a dictionary.

Return Type

- `dict list`

Returns

Returns a `dict` with a single key-value pair. The key is the name of the model's output layer, which is defined by the model you use. The value is a list of `dicts` in which each element is an object that the model identified and its associated probability. The user who applies the model should know how to parse the result.

Example

Sample output:

```
1 {
2     'SoftMax_67': array(
3         [
4             2.41881448e-08,
5             3.57339691e-09,
6             1.00263861e-07,
7             5.40415579e-09,
8             4.37702547e-04,
9             6.16787545e-08
10         ],
11     dtype=float32)
12 }
```

model.parseResult(model_type, raw_infer_result)

Parses the results of some commonly used models, such as classification, SSD, and segmentation models. For customized models, you need to write your own parse functions.

Request Syntax

```
1 import awscam
2 model = awscam.Model(model_topology_file, loading_config)
3 raw_infer_result = model.doInference(video_frame)
4 result = model.parseResult(model_type, raw_infer_result)
```

Parameters

- `model_type`—String that identifies the model type to use to generate the inference. Required.

  Valid values: `classification`, `ssd`, and `segmentation`

- `raw_infer_result`—The output of the function `model.doInference(video_frame)`. Required.

Return Type

- `dict`

Returns

Returns a `dict` with a single key-value pair. The key is the model type. The value is a list of `dicts`, in which each element is an object label and probability calculated by the model.

Example

The output of a classification model might look like the following:

```
1 {"output":[
2     {"label":"318","prob":0.5},
3     {"label":"277","prob":0.3},
4     {"label":"433","prob":0.001",
5     ]
6 }
```

The output of an SDD model contains bounding box information, similar to the following:

```
1 {"output": [
2     {"label": "318", "xmin": 124, "xmax": 245, "ymin": 10, "ymax": 142", "prob": 0.5},
3     {"label": "277", "xmin": 89, "xmax": 166, "ymin": 233, "ymax": 376", "prob": 0.3},
4     ... ...
5     {"label": "433", "xmin": 355, "xmax": 468, "ymin": 210, "ymax": 266", "prob": 0.001}
6     ]
7 }
```

Method awscam.getLastFrame()

Retrieves the latest frame from the video stream. The video streaming runs constantly when the AWS DeepLens is running.

Request Syntax

```
1 import awscam
2 ret, video_frame = awscam.getLastFrame()
```

Parameters

- None

Return Type

- `ret`—A Boolean value (true or false) that indicates whether the call was successful.

- `video_frame`—A numpy.ndarray that represents a video frame.

Document History for AWS DeepLens

The following table describes the additions and changes to documentation for AWS DeepLens.

- **API version:** 2017-08-31
- **Latest documentation update:** March 13, 2018

Change	Description	Date
Gluon support	AWS DeepLens adds support for Gluon models. For more information, see Gluon Models.	March 13, 2018
Importing from Amazon SageMaker	AWS DeepLens simplifies the process for importing a model trained with Amazon SageMaker. For more information, see Importing Your Amazon SageMaker Trained Model.	February 22, 2018
Model optimization	AWS DeepLens adds support for optimizing your custom model so that it runs on the GPU instead of the CPU. For more information, see: [See the AWS documentation website for more details]	January 31, 2018
New guide	This is the first release of the AWS DeepLens Developer Guide.	November 29, 2017

AWS Glossary

For the latest AWS terminology, see the AWS Glossary in the *AWS General Reference*.